T0012470

AMERICAN ANALECTS

ALSO BY GARY YOUNG

BOOKS

American Analects / 2024
That's What I Thought / 2018
Even So: New and Selected Poems / 2012
Pleasure / 2006
No Other Life / 2005
Braver Deeds / 1999
Days / 1997
The Dream of a Moral Life / 1990
Hands / 1979

TRANSLATIONS

Taken to Heart: 70 Poems from the Chinese (with Yanwen Xu) / 2022
Precious Mirror, translations from the Japanese / 2018

ANTHOLOGIES (WITH CHRISTOPHER BUCKLEY)

One for the Money: The Sentence as a Poetic Form / 2012
Bear Flag Republic: Prose Poems and Poetics from California / 2008
The Geography of Home: California's Poetry of Place / 1999

LIMITED EDITIONS

Red Cedar, Red Pine / 2022
In the Face of It / 2009
III × III (with Christopher Buckley and Derek McKown) / 2007
No Harm Done / 2004
The Body's Logic / 2000
My Place Here Below / 1996
Then It Happens / 1996
My Brother's in Wyoming / 1994
Wherever I Looked / 1993
Nine Days: New York / 1991
A Single Day / 1991
The Geography of Home / 1987
In the Durable World / 1985
6 Prayers / 1984

American Analects

Poems Gary Young

A KAREN & MICHAEL BRAZILLER BOOK

PERSEA BOOKS / NEW YORK

Copyright © 2024 by Gary Young

All rights reserved. No part of this publication may be reproduced or transmitted in any form or by any means, electronic or mechanical, including photocopy, audio recording, or any information storage and retrieval system, without prior permission in writing from the publisher. Request for permission or for information should be addressed to the publisher:

Persea Books, Inc.
90 Broad Street
New York, New York 10004

LIBRARY OF CONGRESS CATALOGING-IN-PUBLICATION DATA

Names: Young, Gary, 1951– author.
Title: American analects : poems / Gary Young.
Description: New York : Persea Books, 2024. | "A Karen & Michael Braziller book." | Summary: "From Gary Young, master of the prose poem, this moving collection reflects upon the death of a beloved mentor, a parent, and friends—both before and during the COVID-19 pandemic"— Provided by publisher.
Identifiers: LCCN 2024004167 (print) | LCCN 2024004168 (ebook) | ISBN 9780892555925 (paperback ; acid-free paper) | ISBN 9780892555932 (e-pub)
Subjects: LCSH: Death—Poetry. | LCGFT: Poetry.
Classification: LCC PS3575.O785 A84 2024 (print) | LCC PS3575.O785 (ebook) | DDC 811/.54—dc23/eng/20240209
LC record available at https://lccn.loc.gov/2024004167
LC ebook record available at https://lccn.loc.gov/2024004168

Book design and composition by Rita Skingle
Typeset in Garamond Premier
Manufactured in the United States of America. Printed on acid-free paper.

This book is dedicated to the memory of
Gene Holtan and Elizabeth Sanchez

CONTENTS

The Master said,
"Words are all you need to get your point across."

THE ANALECTS OF CONFUCIUS, BOOK XV, NO. 41

Follow the instructions to the door.
When you get to the door, throw the instructions away.

—GENE HOLTAN, LAST WORDS

AMERICAN ANALECTS

Last night I fell asleep, and in a dream, I wrote a poem. I worked every line into place, and when I'd finished, I woke up, scribbled the poem down in the dark, and went back to sleep. In the morning, I picked up the notepad beside my bed expecting to find the poem, but there was only a single word printed there: *snow.* The authentic self is inarticulate, and there is no end to the excitement of failure.

Gene was always thinking, and he thought out loud. I loved his voice, and the lavish alchemy of his mind. He said, defensiveness keeps us from finding out what really *is*. The wonder is that when we allow ourselves to see what's real, it doesn't damage us. We both watched a mockingbird in a crabapple outside the window. Gene said, what I haven't thought of yet is always better than what I'm thinking now.

My younger son considers the effect of imaginary numbers on imaginary numbers. His brother ponders the duality of abstraction and specificity, while I wrestle with the concept of essential nature. We are pilgrims. The branch of a willow bounces off its reflection on the surface of a canal. Mallards bob in a murky pond. A crow tears at the body of a mouse on the gray tile roof of a temple.

Gene said, it's impossible to be honest with yourself; it isn't achievable for anyone. The world is incomprehensible, and our defenses defeat us. I asked him, isn't there anything we can believe in? Of course, he said, but it should be something arbitrary. He gazed out the window—ah, clouds.

The temple opens onto a garden and a stream, and below a room hung with portraits of thirty-six immortal poets, a frog blurts out a poem of his own. He knows everything he needs to know about immortality. Tadpoles rest in the mud at the bottom of the stream, and a wagtail flitting over the garden leaves a white dropping on the glassy leaf of a gardenia.

A plum tree appeared between the woods and what's left of the orchard, the seed either spit out, or dropped there in coyote scat. A redwood limb came down in a storm once, and tore the tree in half, but it grew back, and erupts in a cloud of white blossoms every spring. For years I've promised to prune it and rein it in, but I'm too lazy, or too old, and I've let it grow wild. The blossoms last a week unless a late storm blows in and strips the tree bare.

In the hills above Kyoto, the hut that Buson built on the ruin of Bashō's home still stands. Its thatched roof staves off rain, thunder rattles the paper screens in the windows, and bamboo trembles in the wind. Poems are still being written there beside the silent graves.

Gene once confessed that when he was younger, he'd had a terrible temper, and often flew into a rage. I couldn't imagine it; I had never seen him the least bit angry. Gene said, after my wife died, my anger left me. He said, she hadn't been the source of my anger, but when she was gone, anger was one of many things that died in me.

Each night, an owl cries out from the redwoods. He calls, and I call back. I call, and he answers. We share the same bright moon, the same shadows, and the same fate. The possibility of discussion is limitless; we have no secrets. This morning I discovered an owl pellet by the front door—a wad of fur, and a jumble of femurs and little ribs—oracle bones, easy to decipher.

Yesterday we sat on the bank of the Kamo River, laughing and drinking beer. Today, that very spot collapsed into swollen floodwaters. In the temples, there is so much talk about emptiness, and the ground of being. The void in the riverbank is large enough to hold us all.

For Gene, the authority of mark-making was a comfort. He said, it's exhilarating to be available to your own inquiry, to create your own map, to say, this is me. It's of no use to the others, and it can't be explained. That's its value.

I found half a robin's egg beneath a maple tree. I don't know if a chick was hatched and the shell fell from the nest, or if a jay found the egg and this is all that's left. The shell just fits over my fingertip, a pale blue thimble, like the sky pressing down from above.

Betsy Minter woke one morning with a cough, and three days later she was dead. We met when we were children, but it was decades before I learned that from the time she was twelve, she and her mother played Hearts and drank beer every afternoon while they waited for her father to come home from work. Sixty years ago, her father taught me how to fish. This morning, I fished for hours. I took my hat off when I came in from the water, but for the rest of the day, I couldn't shake the sensation that it was still on my head.

When consciousness confronts the true self, which has no voice, the most natural response is to make a mark. Gene said, every mark tells a story—*is* a story. We have to find that inarticulate space outside of language and wander around there. It's a void that needs to be peopled, an endless opportunity for the unexpected. Being irrelevant to any existing need is a liberating place to find oneself.

You don't need much to attract sugar ants: honey crusted on the lid of a jar, a single grain of sugar that falls from a spoon, and an army will parade across your kitchen floor or up the cupboards until they reach whatever draws them. When our boys were still children, I loved to lean over them as they slept, to smell their sweet breath. It tethered us, every breath a link in a chain.

A killing heat beat the birds into silence. A single cicada called from a ginkgo but got no reply. At the fish market, mackerel, tuna, and octopus floated in tubs of ice. Vegetables bobbed beside them in the slushy mix. A woman at the stall filled a bag with ice, balanced it on her head, and put both hands to her mouth so she could laugh at herself.

My body does not belong to me. Lying motionless for an MRI, the magnetic coils grind away, searching for tumors. I imagine little seeds of death floating all around us. The hypnotic machine pulses and whines, and I'm in the monastery, meditating while cicadas electrify the stagnant air. A monk beats on a wooden drum, and the imaging machine speeds up. The monk whispers, still yourself, and the technician says, you're almost through.

I saw a snowy egret standing on a mat of kelp, bobbing with the swells and the tide. There were sailboats, fog on the far side of the bay, a little chop beyond the point. When I told Gene, he said, it's an astonishment that each day is different from another, that things are inconsistent day-to-day.

My brother's barber was an alcoholic, but he only drank every other year—one year drunk, the next year sober. I asked my brother if the haircuts his barber gave him sober were better than the ones he gave when he was drunk, and my brother insisted there was no difference. His barber died in the pandemic, and my brother was surprised by how shaken he had been. My brother said, it was like losing two friends at once.

When I lived in town, I often dreamed that I'd buried a body behind my house, and I'd wake terrified that someone would discover it. The house was an old Victorian, and a man once came to the door to ask if he could search for treasure in my backyard. He carried a steel rod five feet long, with a handle at one end. We use these probes to locate murder victims and mass graves, he said, but I'm just looking for old trash pits. He drove the rod into the ground, feeling for a change in density. He dug up bottles, broken plates, then his probe hit something unyielding, and he pulled up a tin box filled with the skeleton of a dog. He wanted to keep it, but I put the box back in the hole and packed it tight with earth.

Gene said, if your ideas are good enough, your students will carry them forward. An old student of mine once showed me a beautiful, handbound book filled with notes she'd taken in my class. She opened it and read: *Our devotion is to truth, not to facts. You compete against the dead for the attention of the unborn. Inability is where genius flowers.*

Paradise is burning. The woods, the homes, the people inside them all rise, and are carried off on the wind. A dark cloud skirts the coastal range, slips through the gaps between peaks, and settles over us. Our eyes water, and our lungs catch. We know what we're breathing—every breath is a burial.

I write poems with my sons, while Buson lies in his grave just a few steps away.

When I stare into the well beside Buson's grave, rain disturbs the surface of the water. A face is reflected there, but whose?

This morning, I was playing poker in a dream, and a nuthatch sitting next to me said, this game's too rich for my blood, and flew away. Then I woke, and heard the dawn chorus, every bird in the canyon trilling and chirping at once. I used to believe their songs meant, *here I am!* Now I think they're saying, *where am I?*

Jon Veinberg plays bocce in heaven. The clacking balls make celestial music, winos draped in white robes sip Chardonnay, and stray dogs gnaw on meaty bones. There's Armenian flatbread, platters of blood sausage, and Czechoslovakian beer to wash it all down. A choir in the clouds sings the blues, but here, where the rain keeps falling, crows circle overhead and refuse to land.

Gene believed there's virtue in being incidental and embracing the achieved accident of who you are. I'm not so sure. Fruit ripening on the branches of the apricot and plum promise sweetness; it's easy to forget that within each tender fruit, there's a stone at its core.

I was never sure what was going on inside my father. I tried talking to him, but he never listened to anything he didn't want to hear. Still, the last time we spoke, he said, I had the strangest dream. It was like a story, not just terrifying little bursts. I've never had a dream like that before. I don't remember exactly what I said to him, but just before he died, he left a message on my answering machine: You mean nothingness is a *thing?*

A Buddha large as a mountain sits motionless, while the mountain behind it shudders in a warm breeze that rustles the pine, bamboo, and cedar clinging to its slopes.

When Gene decided to devote himself to painting, he took his prints, and dumped them at the landfill. A dozer was pushing them into a large pile of refuse when the driver said, hold on, that looks like real art, and pulled them out of the trash heap. Gene had never been prouder; it was the best review he'd ever received. Gene said, art is outside of purpose. You take what you need without knowing that you're taking it, and without knowing that it's what you needed.

As the weather warms year after year, aspens move higher up the draws, and the mesas are green into September. Eagles hunt over Red Canyon, hawks keep watch in the pines, and ospreys dip into the streams. It is late in the season when the waxwings gorge themselves on chokecherries, lift as one, spin above the hay fields, and head for the prairie.

Fleeing the oncoming storm, a heron, like a hungry ghost, passed so close that its wings lifted the hair on my head.

Stanley Fullerton was an artist and a fisherman. I loved his self-portraits—always in a slouch hat, a pipe in his mouth, and a fish under his arm. Stan collaged nautical creatures out of scraps, and made etching plates from torn bits of netting and tattered rope. When he was a soldier in Korea, he stepped on a land mine and was blown apart. It took two years in a hospital to piece him back together. Stan's figures were always a little clumsy, and looked bemused, as if they could hardly imagine their good fortune to be rendered whole.

A vulture flew past my window, and when I went outside to look, there were a dozen of them teetering overhead. I followed them to a clearing in the woods, where they tore at the carcass of a deer. When I approached, the vultures flapped their enormous, baggy wings, and retreated to branches just out of reach. Their feathers sounded like bolts of silk being sawed in half, and they sat there, dark priests of a fearsome religion. They feasted until the sun had set, and when they rose and drifted off, their crimson heads glowed like jewels.

A mountain, an island, an ocean made of white stones. Red pine, red cedar, and maple on the farther shore. The gate that leads to this garden is locked from the inside. The Buddha waits just beyond.

My wife found two quail eggs beneath a woodpile being fed into a chipper. The eggs were powder blue with confetti spots the color of chocolate. The shells looked solid, but when she held them, they trembled and throbbed. She put them in a cardboard box lined with wool and placed them under a lamp. Days went by, then weeks, and at last my wife put the lamp away and set the tiny eggs on a shelf.

Gene insisted that the real cannot be measured, that whatever relies on scale is false. He said, we wrestle with an inability to mine ourselves; it's difficult to do, though in your poems you've found a way to do it. The clarity of the interior can't be suppressed. *The moon stacks its dishes in the sink.*

The morning Rick Roberts died, his wife handed him a glass of water, left the room for just a moment, and when she returned, he was dead, the glass still in his hand. Rick and I met every Friday for forty years, a pendulum that punctuated the chaos of the week. He was a fatalist, imperfect, virtuous. The last time I saw him, I kissed him on his cheek. I'd had no idea that his beard was so soft.

Cormorants gather on a mudstone spire, and a blade of kelp backlit by afternoon light curls and twists in a glassy wave. Field hands silhouetted against the sea ride their mud-caked bikes from row to row laying pipe, and in the distance, cattle graze on the rocky bluffs. The Santa Lucias seem to float on the cold current welling up from the canyon beneath the bay, while clouds at dusk turn the water lavender and plum, the light captured by the swells as backwash swallows each incoming wave.

Two monks in white robes climb to the top of Mount Inari. They pass through 10,000 torii gates and stop at a hundred shrines. At every shrine they empty coins from an offering box into a wooden crate that one of the monks carries on his back. For him, the walk down the mountain is harder than the walk up.

Gene was talking to a man on the street, and later said, I recognized his face as he spoke, but I'd forgotten his name. Thankfully, he started telling me stories about himself, and they reminded me who he was.

Back in Wyoming, I ride the trails I rode as a boy. The meadowlark and the vireo sing as they once did, and clouds billow over Stone Mountain. It's warm, but the blossoms on the bindweed are so thick you could mistake them for snow. Horses die, and new horses take their place, but the names—Ginger, Banjo, Lightning—never change. I fish the same streams, walk the same paths, but at the end of my arms, an old man's hands.

It's possible to enter the Great Buddha of Kamakura, to feel the sheets of bronze from the inside, and gaze into the Buddha's head. The metal sings when you strike it with your hand, and the world falls away. Like the body of an aircraft, the metal skin holds off catastrophe. When you exit at last, there's no telling where you might be.

Gene said, the idea of an appropriate object of interest holds no meaning to an artist. The freedom of our availability is outside the demands of the tribe. I have no reason to protest my position; the world is infinite—it can be reconsidered.

Benjamin Britten was so appalled by the horrors of the First World War he was given exemption from military service when war broke out again. While Britten was writing his opera, *The Rape of Lucretia,* my father was patrolling off the coast of Saipan. My father had been dead for a week when I heard Britten's *Phantasy Quartet,* and I sat so close to the musicians that I might have reached out and touched them.

The children playing tag on the riverbank chase one another beside the swift water, and don't notice the pair of kites snatching sparrows from the bead trees overhead.

Gene said, how is it that the three of us had such strong, shared feelings? Elizabeth believed that biology was all about pleasure, and everything else mere annoyances diverting us from the pleasures we were born to, and you agreed. The clarity of her thought could purify the air around us. I gave choice over to her suggestions, or I regretted my resistance. Seeing things with my own eyes for the first time in thirty years is not reassuring. I was loved and I knew it. For me that was an accomplishment—not being loved, but knowing that I was.

An elderly woman and her daughter sat side-by-side while we waited in the airport for a flight. The daughter was knitting a child's cap out of pink yarn, and when the line went taut, she pulled another length from a skein lying between them. As she tugged, and tugged again, I couldn't look away from the needles and the intricate knots. The old woman smiled at me and said, it seems to go on forever, but it really takes no time at all.

Cranes follow the river north toward the mountains at dusk, and though they cry out as they go, we cannot hear them over the roar of the river flooded with this afternoon's rain.

Gene said, a love affair in old age is what the world is all about. Everything is more expanded—you find yourself surprised to have feelings that you didn't have the day before, and you discover new ones every day. He said, when Elizabeth died, the vacancy was overwhelming; I couldn't recognize the world. Things are very still here, he said. The stillness of impossibility is one thing, but this stillness is everywhere. He said, lately there's been a change: Elizabeth is becoming a reference point rather than a reality, and her absence is oppressive, unbearable. I have her pans, her hat, but I want Elizabeth back.

Venus appears above a thumbnail moon. The stars, not yet visible, burn in space. A pink cloud rests on the horizon, lit by the sun that has dropped below the skyline. A heavy mist dulls the moon as a fog bank nestles gray on gray.

In line at the market, an old woman leaving the store caught my eye. Gray-haired and frail, she looked familiar, though for my life I couldn't place her. Then it struck me that I had slept with her once, when we were both young. I watched her vanish through the door, while I stood there, waiting to check out.

Gene kept painting after Elizabeth died, but said, I've lost my audience. He said, at least I haven't lost interest in a conversation with the work, but there's no reason for doing it, and who's doing it is unknown to me.

At the end of a narrow, cobbled lane, crows gorge on sweet fruit at the top of an orange tree and leave nothing but an empty rind that hangs there like a waning moon.

A year after fire tore through the mountains, the redwoods that survived showered everything with seeds. They lay in drifts against the house, smothered the ponds, and clogged the gutters and the creek. Juncos and chickadees gorged on them, but now, after a hard rain, they're all sprouting at once—in terracotta pots, cracks in the pavement, in the joints of stone walls. In my flower beds, they're thick as a lawn, a soft green mat of redwoods already competing for the light. I kneel and wipe away the little forest with my hand.

Gene said, whenever I read a book, I always tell Elizabeth what I think of it, and she responds. I hear her voice, not in my head, but in my ears, out of the air. I talk to her all the time; the neighbors think I'm crazy. I don't know how long this will last, how long she'll speak, but I worry that someday her voice will be gone.

Flowers, cups of sake and cans of beer have been left for the dead, and candle stubs rest on rusty iron spikes. New gravestones made of polished granite glisten. Prayers, and the names of the dead have been deeply etched; it seems they will last forever. Higher up the mountain, the graves are older, more elaborate, and near the peak, three emperors and their retinues lie buried. The names are barely legible. The rain and the moss never tire.

When Gene could no longer hold a brush, he moved into a small house without a studio. One of his old paintings filled the wall above the kitchen table, and I would study it whenever we sat there and talked. Gene's work encouraged contingency and interruption. When lines or fields of color collided, he embraced the unexpected rupture of his intentions. Gene said, in old age there's no longer a need to defend oneself. The metaphor we create for our own survival is difficult to dismantle, but not impossible. He said, I know that this is a prelude to dying, but the vapor of imagination is intoxicating, and the days indescribably beautiful. From my seat, I could see the slips of paper that Gene had taped to all the cabinets in his kitchen. One said, *plates,* another, *bowls,* and on the silverware drawer, *silverware.*

The house finch is a personable bird. He shares the feeder and moves if he is nudged. When other birds scatter, he stays put, unperturbed. He sings at sunrise, and he sings at dusk. His song is joyful and reckless. His head is a crimson blaze. That same fire burns in me.

Each moment blossoms, stutters, and takes its place in the past. Bees sip water from the moss at the edge of a pond. Scarlet oaks tremble in a breeze. Night falls. I held Gene's hand while he was dying. He fell asleep, and when he woke, his mouth tightened, and he started to cry. He didn't cry because he was dying, he cried because I was there, and would have to watch him die. Outside, the sea was going up in flames.

Fire still smolders in roots and stumps, and has blown up between burn scars from last year's blaze. On the coast, fishing boats anchor close to shore, their lamps like emeralds on the water that call squid to circle and rise. The world roils and churns beneath us, while overhead, stars are whirling to a tune I can almost hear. The words, I already know.

ACKNOWLEDGMENTS

Grateful acknowledgment is made to the following magazines and anthologies where many of these poems previously appeared, some of them in slightly different form:

Askew: "Jon Veinberg plays bocce in heaven"
The American Journal of Poetry: "A Buddha large as a mountain," "When I stare into the well," "Two monks in white robes," "At the end of a narrow, cobbled lane"
Beltway Poetry Quarterly: "Fire still smolders," "When I lived in town"
Catamaran: "In line at the market," "Gene believed that there's virtue"
Chiron Review: "My youngest son considers"
Cloudbank: "In the hills above Kyoto," "Flowers, cups of sake," "Gene said, a love affair," "Gene said, how is it," "Gene said, whenever I read a book"
Conestoga Zen: "This morning, I was playing poker," "Gene was always talking," "A vulture flew past"
Humana Obscura: "I found half a robin's egg," "As the weather warms"
I-70 Review: "A mountain, an island," "I write poems with my sons," "The children playing tag"
Interlitq: "Cormorants gather," "Venus appears," "The Santa Lucias," "Gene said, it's impossible," "Stanley Fullerton"
Miramar: "A plum tree appeared," "Fleeing the oncoming storm"
New American Writing: "Back in Wyoming," "My brother's barber," "Benjamin Britten was so appalled"
New Letters: "Yesterday we sat on the bank," "Cranes follow the river north," "It's possible to enter"

Red Wheelbarrow: "Paradise is burning," "Betsy Minter," "Gene kept painting," "Gene was talking to a man" "I was never sure," "When Gene could no longer," "When consciousness confronts"

Salt: "The temple opens onto a garden," "Gene once confessed," "A killing heat," "A year after fire tore through," "I saw a snowy egret," "You don't need much sugar," "For Gene, the authority," "Gene insisted"

Spillway: "The house finch is a personable bird"

Willow Springs: "Each moment blossoms," "Last night, I fell asleep"

"My body does not belong to me" first appeared in *The Eloquent Poem: 128 Contemporary Poems and their Making,* Persea Books, 2019.

"Each night, an owl cries out" first appeared in *The Plume Anthology of Poetry 9,* MadHat Press, 2021.

"Each moment blossoms" and "Yesterday we sat on the bank" first appeared in *Alcatraz: An International Anthology of Prose/ Poetry,* Life Before Man, New South Wales, Australia, 2022.

"The morning Rick Roberts died," "An elderly woman and her daughter," "When Gene decided," and "My wife found two quail eggs" first appeared in *Dreaming Awake: New Prose Poetry from the United States, Australia, and England,* MadHat Press, 2022.

"My younger son considers" appeared in *Adult Children,* Wising Up Press, 2022.

Many of these poems appeared in *Red Cedar, Red Pine,* the Blue Light Poetry Prize Chapbook Winner, Blue Light Press, 2022.